# my mantra
# is your mantra

## ash nave

### illustration by emily hartung

*A light shone on every path you crossed, Brie.*
Thank you for all the wisdom and humor.
Your words have changed my life forever.

"Only by loving and accepting yourself can you
truly be and express what you are."

– Don Miguel Ruiz

# self-love

# Love is possible,
even when it feels impossible.

I embrace my flaws
with the warmth of the sun.

The more love I give to myself,
the more love I can give to others.

I accept the storm inside me
with gentle thoughts.

I will be kind to myself

because I deserve it.

15

# Today I am strong.
Tomorrow I am stronger.

# When I show compassion to my pain,

my pain becomes compassion.

I am allowed to set boundaries.
Period.

# Every act of kindness
is an act of kindness towards oneself.

# I am not alone.
### I always have me.

# My broken pieces deserve patience,

not frustration.

# Asking for help
# may not be easy,

but it's worth it.

# I am trying my best.
And my best is good enough.

# I want to see my goodness
the way others see my goodness.

# I am making progress,
## not perfection.

It's okay to make mistakes.
It's not okay to not judge myself for them.

I am not guilty of situations
out of my control.

Just because others hurt me
doesn't mean I deserve this pain.

I am not my trauma.
I am a survivor of the past.

# My intuition is the friend I need
when I need clarity the most.

inner peace

# My anxiety is a wave crashing on the shore.
Soon it will drift back out to sea.

I am here in this moment.
I am present with myself.

I am grounded like the earth
beneath my feet.

35

I am calm like a cloud
drifting above the sea.

I let my dark thoughts
pass through me
without judgment.

# Today I choose calm.
Today I choose inner peace.

38

I am not my thoughts,
my thoughts are not me.

# I am allowed to create space between myself

and the negativity around me.

I am strong.
I am patient.
I am capable of riding out this storm.

I cannot change the past,
but I can change right now
by staying present.

42

My anxiety wants to help me,
not hurt me.

# The most beautiful things in life
are imperfect, like the mind.

# When I stop judging my bad thoughts,

I start loving my broken pieces.

45

# It's okay to have bad days.
## Remember that.

46

I am present in this moment.
I am connected to myself
and my surroundings.

# I have the power
# to stay grounded,

so grounded I will be.

I give myself permission
to let go of toxic people

because I don't deserve
the pain they cause me.

# I am protecting my energy
by taking time to rest.

50

I throw judgments of myself
into the ocean
and watch them sink like stones.

# When I need time for myself,

I don't need to give an excuse for that.

# self-motivation

54

If life was meant to be easy,
would it be worth fighting for?

# When I believe in myself,
I am capable of anything.

# Every obstacle
# is an opportunity
to become a better version of myself.

I am here
because I made the
choice to live.

Let me repeat that…

I am stronger
than the hand I've been dealt.

# Happiness is achieved when
I fight for my happiness.

# My darkness is strong.
## My heart is even stronger.

# I won't heal overnight
but I will heal over time.

Not every day is a good day,
but I can do something good for myself
every day.

# Falling down is an opportunity
to find the strength to get back up again.

I choose the mindset
that will help me,
not hurt me.

# This is a simple task,

a simple task I can do.

The mind is a garden and every thought is a seed planting something new.

So I will plant something beautiful.

# When it rains it pours,
so go outside and dance in the rain.

68

If everything feels impossible,
I can always start with what's possible.

69

# The more I chase my dreams,
the more real my dreams become.

I choose to live my life
right now
because tomorrow
doesn't exist

until it's today.

I won't stop until I am proud
of how far I've come.

The more I step into the light,
the more I step away from the dark.

73

There are
good people in my life
who want to see me
at my best.

One of them is me.

www.ingramcontent.com/pod-product-compliance
Lightning Source LLC
Chambersburg PA
CBHW032256070726
47590CB00016B/2949